MATH-A-MAGIC
Number Tricks for Magicians

Laurence B. White, Jr. and Ray Broekel • Illustrated by Meyer Seltzer

Albert Whitman & Company, Morton Grove, Illinois

The authors dedicate this book to Bill White. When he was in school, he liked numbers so much he went to college and became a mathematician.

They also thank James Donovan for his insight into the world of math and its mysteries.

Other books by Laurence B. White, Jr. and Ray Broekel

Abra-Ca-Dazzle: Easy Magic Tricks
Hocus Pocus: Magic You Can Do
Razzle Dazzle! Magic Tricks for You
Shazam! Simple Science Magic

Library of Congress Cataloging-in-Publication Data

White, Laurence B.
  Math-a-magic : number tricks for magicians / Laurence B. White and Ray Broekel : illustrated by Meyer Seltzer.
      p.   cm.
  Summary: Provides instructions for twenty magic tricks using numbers, with explanations of the mathematics behind each trick.
  ISBN 0-8075-4994-0
  1. Mathematical recreations. [1. Mathematical recreations.
2. Magic tricks.] I. Broekel, Ray. II. Seltzer, Meyer, ill.
III. Title.
QA95. W58 1990
793.8–dc20   89-35395
                                      CIP
                                        AC

CONTENTS

GETTING STARTED

You've heard of a mathematician. And you've heard of a magician. Well, this book is going to turn you into both of these people—you will become a math-a-magician!

Why Math and Magic?

People have always been fascinated by numbers and what they do. Almost as soon as numbers were invented and put to work, we began to use them for play as well. Math and fun just naturally go together! Think of all the games you like to do that need numbers just to work right. Some games are almost nothing *but* numbers: dice, card games, hopscotch, and board games with play money, to name a few.

Numbers aren't just useful and fun—they have a way of being magical, too. The reason is that they're sensible little guys who know how to behave. Since they always follow certain rules, we can toss them around, mix them with words, hide them, or put them together in strange ways—and they keep on working the way they always do. The same goes for geometry, the kind of math that deals with lines and shapes.

The first time you learned to sing a counting song, or added up a lot of anything, or solved a hard division problem, you might have felt the excitement of math's magic. You probably never thought about it this way, but each thing you learned was a kind of math "trick." And you know a lot more! You learned them in school, on the playground, or in your own living room or kitchen.

Of course, not all of the math magic you know would look good on stage. To be a real math-a-magician, you must choose *the right kind of tricks* and practice them carefully. This book will teach you math magic tricks to perform in front of a group or just your best friend.

Patter's Important

Good magicians have learned that they need to start off their performances with a quick line of patter —entertaining talk—to help keep their audiences on their toes. They also put patter into the rest of the show, in each trick they do. Besides keeping people laughing, patter can distract your audience while you are doing the secret part of a trick. Here is an example of some opening patter:

> Before I begin, I need to have the answer to a riddle I heard. Listen carefully. What has one scoop of vanilla ice cream, one scoop of strawberry ice cream, chocolate sauce, whipped cream, chopped nuts, a cherry, and sharp teeth? Give up? An alligator sundae! Hope you were sharp enough to get that one. Now, let me bedazzle you with my first trick. Originally, I had planned to saw a woman in half for you. She hasn't been able to sew herself back together again from the last show as yet, so I'll do the _____ trick for you right now!

Then start off with the trick of your choice. Get the idea? Use this beginning, or better yet, create your own patter for a great performance. You'll find more examples of patter throughout this book. Remember: patter makes your act seem even better than it is.

Oh, by the way. What do you call rain talk?
Pitter Patter.

IF YOU PUT THREE DUCKS IN A BOX, THEN ANOTHER THREE DUCKS IN THE SAME BOX, WHAT WOULD YOU HAVE? A BOX OF QUACKERS!

5

A SURE BET

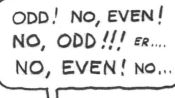

The Trick

Want to win a penny from a friend with a sure bet that she can't win? Just put a dime, a nickel, and four pennies into your pocket, and you're set.

"Do you like to win money? Do you have a penny?" you ask your friend. As she fishes for the penny, you reach into your own pocket and take out the coins. Rattle them in your fist, but don't let your friend see them.

Then say, "I've got more than a penny in my hand, as you can hear. You have a penny in your hand. That's only *one* coin, so it's an *odd* number. I call this my 'Odd or Even' bet." Then ask, "If you were to add your odd penny to the coins in my hand, do you think all of it together would be an odd or an even number?"

Whatever your friend says, you say, "Will you bet your penny on being right? If you are wrong I keep your penny, but if you are right you keep *all* of my change!"

It sounds like a good bet for your friend, doesn't it? After all, she has a fifty/fifty chance of winning, right? Wrong! Your friend will always lose!

How to Do It

If your friend guesses "odd," you simply open your hand, add her penny to the coins, and total their money value. That will be twenty cents, which is an *even* number. If your friend guesses "even," you open your hand, add the penny, and count the number of coins. There will be seven coins, which is an *odd* number! You win!

6

The Math-a-Magic Secret

You, the magician, stay in control because you're the one who does the counting. You count either the number of coins or the money value of the coins, depending on whether you need an odd or even result to win the bet. As long as you have altogether an *odd number of coins* whose money value adds up to an *even number of cents*, you can't lose. In fact, the math of this trick also works if you have an even number of coins with an odd money value. Just remember that the number of coins—odd or even—must be different from the money value of the coins—even or odd.

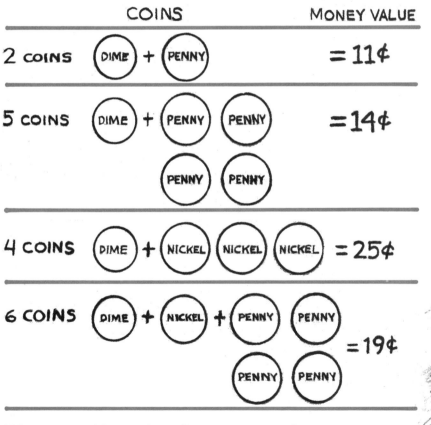

	COINS	MONEY VALUE
2 COINS	DIME + PENNY	= 11¢
5 COINS	DIME + PENNY PENNY PENNY PENNY	= 14¢
4 COINS	DIME + NICKEL NICKEL NICKEL	= 25¢
6 COINS	DIME + NICKEL + PENNY PENNY PENNY PENNY	= 19¢

When you add your friend's *one* coin worth *one* cent you are simply adding *one* to both sides of the chart above. (Just for fun, try to figure out more combinations of even-odd coins!)

I KEEP LOSING!
IT MUST BE A
COININCIDENCE!

7

TAP AN ANIMAL

The Trick

Here is a simple trick to try on a friend. Draw the chart for this trick on a piece of paper and carry it with you. Whenever a friend says, "Show me some magic," you can say, "I'm too lazy, but if you want to do some yourself, try this."

Here's what to tell your friend: "First, secretly choose the name of one of the animals on the chart. Now, tap out its name with your fingertip, letter by letter. Make your first tap on the circle in the center, the one that says 'start here,' while silently saying the first letter of your animal's name. Follow the arrows to the rattlesnake, and tap this as you say the second letter of your chosen animal. Follow the arrows to the cat and tap that for the third letter. Continue following the arrows, tapping each animal you meet as you say the next letter of your secret animal's name."

When your friend stops tapping, you'll be able to tell her what animal she chose! How? *Her finger will be resting right on that animal's name!* She can try thinking of a different animal and, starting at the center circle, tap its name again, letter by letter. But she will always magically end by pointing her finger at her chosen animal.

How to Do It

It is very important that you copy the chart for this trick exactly (but you don't need to draw the animals' pictures). The trick works with arithmetic; the number of letters in each animal's name is important. If you wish to change an animal's name you may do so, but you must change it to an animal whose name has the same number of letters. For example, you could change CAT, which has three letters, to RAT or APE or DOG, which also have three letters. The trick then works itself—as your friend taps one name after another, she is also *counting*.

The Math-a-Magic Secret

None of the animals has a name with only one or two letters in it. The first tap (number one) is at the center, and the second tap (number two) is at the RATTLESNAKE. Now, the tricky part happens, at the third tap. Here, there's an animal's name that has *three* letters (CAT). If someone thought of CAT, after three taps they would be pointing at its name. Four taps brings them to BULL, a name with four letters. Each following animal has a name made of the same number of letters as the number of taps it takes to reach it:

MOUSE – 5   KANGAROO – 8   RATTLESNAKE –11
MONKEY – 6   BLUE WHALE – 9
RACCOON – 7   SALAMANDER –10

Once you learn the secret, you can make up other tap tricks like this one. Try making one using the names of people, or different colors, or common objects, like PEN, DOOR, RULER, PENCIL.

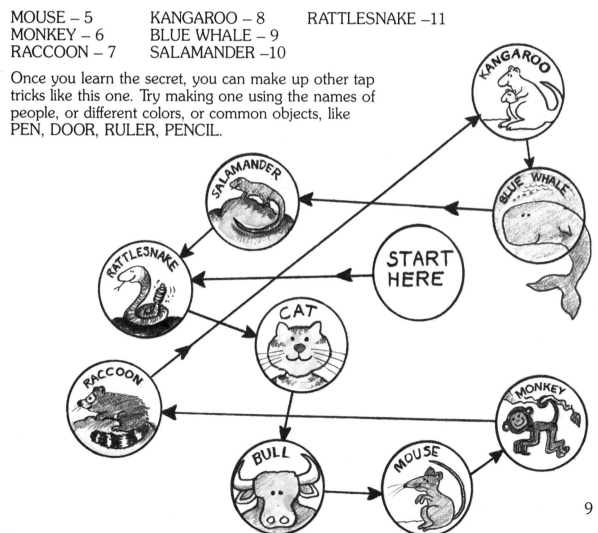

9

HEADS AND TAILS

The Trick

If you try this trick right now, it will fool you. Then, try it on your friends and fool *them*!

You will need twelve coins of any value and a copy of the drawing on page 11. Place the coins, one in each box, on the drawing. Now do the following things:

1 Turn the coins so they *all* show either heads or tails. You decide which.

2 Turn over the following coins: numbers 1, 3, 4, 5, 8, and 10.

3 Now, turn over *any six* coins you choose. You can even turn over any or all of the coins you just turned over. Now for the magic . . .

4 Push the following coins out of the boxes (Don't turn them over as you do this!): numbers 9, 11, 12, 6, 2, and finally . . . 7.

And the trick is done! What was the trick, you ask? Well, look carefully at the heads and tails of the coins. You will find you have pushed out the same number of heads and the same number of tails as you have left in the boxes! And it made no difference which coins you turned over in step number three!

How to Do It

Just make a drawing of the boxes and number them. Then, memorize the steps. That way, you can do the trick for your friends without even looking at the coins. You'll soon convince them you are a great magician!

10

The Math-a-Magic Secret

Let's assume we started this trick with all twelve coins heads up. After step 2, the coins numbered 1, 3, 4, 5, 8, and 10 will be all tails up. The other six coins—2, 6, 7, 9, 11, and 12—are all heads right now. These are the ones which your friend will push out of the boxes later.

Although it's not obvious to anyone but you, the six coins that will be pushed out are *all heads* and the six that stay in place are *all tails*. Let's think of them as two separate groups:

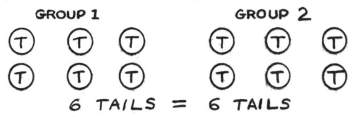

GROUP 1
COINS TO BE PUSHED

GROUP 2
COINS THAT STAY IN

Now, in step 3, any six coins may be turned over. If your friend turns over *all* of group 1:

GROUP 1   GROUP 2

6 TAILS = 6 TAILS

If he or she turns over 5 of group 1 and 1 of group 2:

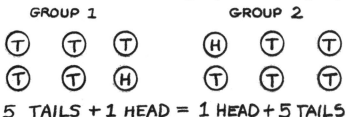

GROUP 1   GROUP 2

5 TAILS + 1 HEAD = 1 HEAD + 5 TAILS

You can see now that no matter which six coins get turned over, the trick works. The coins that are pushed out will look the same as the ones that aren't!

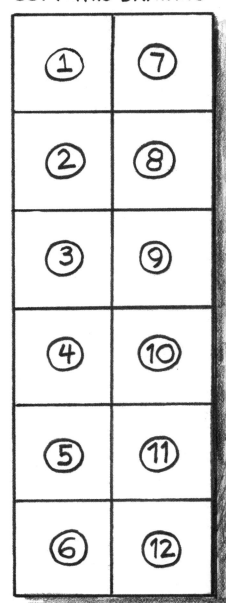

COPY THIS DRAWING

①	⑦
②	⑧
③	⑨
④	⑩
⑤	⑪
⑥	⑫

FAVORITE NUMBERS

11, 12, 13, 14, 15 AND 16.

The Trick

"In this trick," you tell your friend, "*you* get to be the magician." You place a deck of cards and a folded piece of paper on the table. "I've got a favorite card, and it's written on this piece of paper. You don't know what that card is, but with my magic to help you, you're going to find out. First, though, I need to know something. My favorite number is sixteen. What's your favorite number, between one and ten?" Let's say your helper says, "Ten."

"You didn't know my favorite number, and I didn't know yours, but let's use our numbers to choose a card from this deck. We'll start with your number and go to mine." You begin by saying "ten" as you remove a card from the top of the deck and place it on the table. Another card, "eleven," is taken from the deck and dropped on the table. Then "12, 13, 14, 15, and 16." Card after card is removed as you count out loud, until your favorite number, sixteen, is reached.

"Now," you explain, "use your favorite number again. Beginning with 'one,' count off that many cards from the deck onto the pile." Your friend counts off the ten cards. You ask him to turn the last card (the tenth one) over. It is the four of clubs. "You did it!" you say. "You really *are* a magician!" You turn the folded paper over. It says, "four of clubs."

How to Do It

This trick requires some preparation before your audience is present. (Because of this, you'll only be able to do it one time for any one performance.) First, decide on your "favorite number." It can be any number between 11 and 51. Then, simply count that number off the top of the deck and remember the *next* card. Write the name of this card on the paper as your favorite card. Then put all the cards back into the deck exactly the way they were. When you ask for your helper's favorite number, be sure it's between *one* and *ten*, so that it is smaller than yours.

The Math-a-Magic Secret

Pretend you are counting a dozen doughnuts. You would start with the first one and go on to twelve. *But*, you could also start with the *eighth* one and count, "8, 9, 10, 11, 12," and then *go back to the first one and count*, "*1, 2, 3, 4, 5, 6, 7*." It's crazy—but it's still a dozen!

That is very close to what goes on here. You know the seventeenth card is the four of clubs. So you say that your favorite number is sixteen. Your helper says, "ten." You begin by counting cards, saying "10, 11, 12, 13, 14, 15, 16." Your helper then counts, "1, 2, 3, 4, 5, 6, 7, 8, 9, 10." You can see now that you and your helper have counted out seventeen cards in the same crazy way you counted the twelve doughnuts.

DO YOU KNOW HOW TO DIVIDE 16 APPLES EQUALLY BETWEEN 10 CHILDREN?

MAKE APPLESAUCE!

AROUND THE SQUARE

SQUARES ARE JUST CIRCLES WITH CORNERS.

The Trick

"Let's play a magical game of charades," you tell your audience. "I'll act out a sentence, word by word, and you have to figure out what I am saying."

First you point to yourself. Then you make a big letter *M* in the air with your finger. Next, point to one side. Then pick up a ring made of cardboard and hold it up. Point to it. Finally, ask the audience, "What am I saying?"

Your audience, no doubt, will be completely confused. So, you explain. You point to yourself and say, "I." Make the letter M and say, "I am (M)." Point and say, "I am going." Then show the cardboard ring and say, "I am going around." While you are showing the ring, you suddenly "remember." "Oops, I am sorry. I forgot to do my magic trick. What I meant to say was 'I [point to yourself] am [make the M] going [point away] around [show the ring] . . . the square [you suddenly twist the ring and it magically turns into a square]!' Yes, that's it. I am going around the square. Did you get it?"

Suddenly, you look puzzled. "Or, was the square I went a 'round'?" And the square changes instantly back into a ring!

How to Do It

The "round square" is easy to make and is a really fun way to trick people. You will need four equal-length pieces of flexible cardboard strips. Punch holes in both ends of each strip. Then fasten the strips together, end

BRASS FASTENER PUT THROUGH PUNCHED HOLES.

to end, with brass fasteners. When you are done, it will look like a square.

Now, if you hold one side of the square in each hand and move your hands apart, turning them inward as you do, the square will change into a ring.

If you twist the ring, you can change it back into a square instantly. A few minutes of playing and practice and you will catch on. Now you are ready to present this math-a-magical geome-trick to your friends. Just follow the patter and routine that we've suggested, or better still, make up your own!

The Math-a-Magic Secret

This trick uses a kind of geometry called topology, which studies how objects are able to change their shapes but keep their basic characteristics. There are two reasons the object you make in this trick can do what it does: *flexible* pieces of cardboard and *moveable* hinges. They're what allow you to change from a square to a circle, and back again. To a topologist, a circle is only a line going around an empty space—or a square with rounded corners!

15

SILLY FINGER COUNTING

The Trick

Here's a silly trick that's good to begin a show. Spread the fingers of both of your hands and hold them toward your audience. Then say, "Have you noticed? I am one of those few people who has eleven fingers!" And you prove it! Your "proof" won't baffle anyone in the audience, but it will make them *all* laugh.

How to Do It

Hold your left hand up with the fingers spread. Point to your little finger and say, "Let's count backwards. This one is ten." Next, touch your ring finger and say, "nine." Touch your middle finger and say, "eight," then your index finger, as you say, "seven." Finally, point to your thumb, saying, "and this one is six." Then, *immediately* hold up your other hand—with the fingers spread—and say, "*and these five more make eleven!*"

It really surprises people for a moment. Then they catch on—and laugh. Try it!

The Math-a-Magic Secret

If you count the fingers on one hand *backwards*, starting with "ten," you will always finish by saying "six." Then, you can easily confuse your audience by holding up your other hand, showing five fingers, and saying, "and these five fingers make *eleven*!" Everyone knows that 6 + 5 = 11, so your audience will, at least for a moment, be confused by your handy-dandy "backwards" math-a-magic!

16

The Trick

CALCULATOR MAGIC

If you have a pocket calculator, this number trick is quick and simple. If you don't have a calculator, the trick will still work, but you will have to do a lot of multiplying. So, have a sharp pencil!

1   Write, or enter into your calculator, this number: 1 2 3 4 5 6 7 9. Notice that there is no 8 in the sequence.

2   Now, choose a one-digit number and multiply 1 2 3 4 5 6 7 9 by that number. (You can see why it will take a long time to do this with paper and pencil!)

3   Multiply your total by 9. Surprise! Try it again, using a different number in step 2.

How to Do It

This trick practically works by itself. All you have to do is use your pocket calculator and carefully follow the directions above.

The Math-a-Magic Secret

The secret behind this trick is so complicated it would make a math professor dizzy. But *you* have probably already figured out that the magic lies in the number nine. All numbers may be special, but nine is *extra* special. For instance, notice how magical the nines table in the right hand margin is.

It's this amazing way that nines fit together that makes the calculator trick work. Try it with a pencil and paper so you can watch all the "carrying." And, just for fun, try the trick *with* the missing eight included. You'll see the eight causes one small problem. (Don't let your audience see this experiment.)

The Magical 9's Table

$9 \times 1 = 09$

$9 \times 2 = 18$

$9 \times 3 = 27$

$9 \times 4 = 36$

$9 \times 5 = 45$

$9 \times 6 = 54$

$9 \times 7 = 63$

$9 \times 8 = 72$

$9 \times 9 = 81$

THE TENS COLUMN COUNTS UP BY ONES... AND THE ONES COLUMN COUNTS DOWN BY ONES.

MAGIC 9 CALCULATOR

OFF

7

4

1

ON

NOT ONLY THAT, BUT TAKE ANY TOTAL OF THE NINES TABLE, ADD THE DIGITS TOGETHER, AND YOU GET 9!

HOW TO PUT TWELVE PEOPLE IN ELEVEN BEDS

The Trick

This is a wonderful old math-a-magic trick that people have really enjoyed doing. If *you* do it right now, saying the words, you'll know why it's still popular. Maybe you will even fool yourself! Lay eleven coins (or any small objects) in a row, side by side. Ask your audience to pretend that each of the coins is a bed in a hotel and that you are the manager of the hotel.

Now, begin your story: "One night," you say, "I had twelve people come to my hotel, and each one wanted a bed to sleep in. The problem was, as you can see, I had only eleven beds." Point to each coin as you count them out loud, to assure your audience there are only eleven. "But, with a bit of math-a-magic, I was actually able to fit those twelve people into these eleven beds—and everyone got a separate bed!"

Point to the first coin. "To begin, I put two people in the first bed . . . but just for a moment, because I didn't leave them both there." Push the first coin forward a bit to show that it is now "used." Now move the second coin forward and say, "Then I put the *third* person in the *second* bed." Push the third coin forward, saying, "And the *fourth* person in the *third* bed." Continue to push coins forward as you say, "The *fifth* person in the *fourth* bed . . . the *sixth* person in the *fifth* bed . . . the *seventh* person in the *sixth* bed . . . the *eighth* person in the *seventh* bed . . . the *ninth* person in the *eighth* bed . . . the *tenth* person in the *ninth* bed, the *eleventh* person in the *tenth* bed . . . and . . ." You now have one coin remaining in the original row. Push this coin forward and say, "Now I can take the *twelfth* person from the first bed." Pretend to remove the extra person you put in the first bed and place the person on the last coin. "And put the *twelfth* person into the *eleventh* bed!"

You've done it! You seem to have actually put twelve people into eleven beds while your audience watched you closely. But you didn't! You fooled them all!

How to Do It

Simply take eleven coins and lay them out in front of you. Now, read the directions above and do the actions. Once you learn how, just memorize the routine, and you can do it anytime.

The Math-a-Magic Secret

You can't really put twelve people in eleven beds; the secret is that you fool your audience into thinking you do. You fool them with *number words*.

The first two people are put in the first bed. (Remember, these are persons *one* and *two*.) Then you go on until you put the *eleventh* person into the *tenth* bed. You then have one coin left, and the *eleventh bed*. Now, you pretend to take the "extra" person out of the first bed, and you call this person the *twelfth* person. It is *not* the *twelfth* person. It's actually the *second* person, remember? Keep trying until you catch on. You will—but your audience won't!

HOW OLD?

MY MATH-A-MAGICAL POWERS TELL ME THAT OUR TEACHER IS... 93 YEARS OLD!

The Trick

There are many tricks for finding out how old a person is. Usually, someone knows you are doing it with mathematics, but here is a way that will surprise a person. He'll only have to give you a single-digit number!

Give a volunteer a piece of paper and a pencil. Say, "This is an experiment with age. Age has to do with years, and I don't know how many years you have been on the earth. Will you write that figure on the paper without showing it to me?"

You continue: "Age also has to do with months, and there are twelve months in a year. Would you write the number twelve under your age and add the two together?" When he has done this you say, "Age is about days and weeks, too. There are seven days in a week and fifty-two weeks in a year. So write the number 752 and add it to your total." After he has done this, he will expect you to ask for the total, but you surprise him. Have him tell you just the *last digit* of his total. Then, give him his age!

How to Do It

There are two parts to this trick. The first uses mathematics. The second calls upon your guessing abilities (but it's easy).

Here's the math part: Just subtract 4 from the single-digit number the person gives you. (But, if the number he gives you is smaller than 4, you need to "borrow"—add—ten so you can subtract 4.)

The final figure will be the last digit of the person's age.

Now, here's the guessing part: This really is very easy. Look at the person and guess *about* how old he is. Is he in his twenties? thirties? fifties? All you have to do is to be *about* right. Then, simply add that last digit to whatever age you think he is, and you will probably guess correctly. For example, if the person gave you a 7 as the final figure, you simply subtract 4, which gives you 3. Now, look at the person. Does he look 13, or 23, or 33, or 43, or 53, or 63, or 73? You know his age will end in 3, so it won't be very hard to guess.

Oh, one final idea. If you are really having trouble guessing a person's age, always choose the lower number. That way, if you are wrong, your volunteer will at least be flattered that you thought he looked so young!

The Math-a-Magic Secret

This trick uses the big numbers—12 and 752—as a way to distract and confuse your volunteer. The real action takes place in the ones column.

Let's say your volunteer is 55 years old. First, we'll put the person's age into the boxes below:

	HUNDREDS	TENS	ONES
		[5]	[5]
ADD		1	2
ADD	7	5	2
	8	1	(9)

Notice that no matter what number goes into the box in the ones column, you always add 2 and then 2 to it. In the example, the person who is 55 will add 2 and 2 to 5 and tell the magician that his final number is 9. Now, the magician can subtract 4 (the two 2's), know the ones digit, and guess the rest. (Remember, flattery can be a magician's best friend.)

SCHOOL DAZE

I'D REALLY LIKE TO GO TO SCHOOL... THERE'S JUST NOT ENOUGH TIME!

The Trick

Sometimes you can fool people with just a pencil and paper. Try this trick on your teacher or your parents, but here's a warning first: you won't convince anyone that you are right! You'll understand why when you read the directions for this trick.

What this trick tries to do is to prove that you just do not have enough time in a year to go to school. Like the idea? Then get a paper and pencil. Now, say and write what follows:

"There are 365 days in a year, right?" Write 365 on the paper. "I sleep 10 hours a day. This means that, in one year, I am asleep 3,650 hours, which is 152 days." Write

$$\begin{array}{r} 365 \\ -152 \\ \hline 213 \end{array}$$ (days you have left in the year)

"We all know school is not open on weekends, so I can't go to school then. There are 104 Saturdays and Sundays in a year." Write

$$\begin{array}{r} 213 \\ -104 \\ \hline 109 \end{array}$$ (days you now have left)

"And school's not open during summer vacation, which lasts two months, or about 60 days." Write

$$\begin{array}{r} 109 \\ -60 \\ \hline 49 \end{array}$$ (days left)

"And I have to eat every day, and have a little time to play. Altogether that takes about 3 hours a day. That's 45 days worth of hours." Write

$$\begin{array}{r} 49 \\ -45 \\ \hline 4 \end{array}$$ (days left now)

"I haven't even counted holidays, and there are at least 4 of them during the year. So that leaves me with zero days left to go to school!"

We warned you that you probably won't fool anyone with this bit of foolish math-a-magic, but you might surprise someone for a minute or two.

How to Do It

Do it quickly! This is a perfect example of how important patter is to a trick. It is actually what you *say* that fools people. Make each statement sound like a fact, write the numbers on the paper, and immediately begin the next statement. Don't give your audience time to think about the actual arithmetic. Your statements will fool them—the arithmetic won't!

The Math-a-Magic Secret

If this trick still surprises *you*, you'll have to think about it. We are going to leave it for you to puzzle over. But, here's a clue: are there weekends during your summer vacations? Oh, and do you eat, play, and sleep then, too?

IF MY NOSE WERE 12 INCHES LONG... IT WOULD BE A FOOT.

I HAVE A MATHEMATICAL PIECE OF FURNITURE.

WHAT'S IT CALLED?

A MULTIPLICATION TABLE.

23

THE PIANO TRICK

YOU CAN FOOL SOME
OF THE PEOPLE ALL
OF THE TIME!

The Trick

"For this trick," you tell your audience, "I want you to pretend that the table here is a piano." Now, ask a person to come up and place both of her hands palms down on the "piano," fingers out straight and close together. Take two cards and place them together between the person's right thumb and forefinger. Take two more and place them between the forefinger and middle finger.

Continue to place pairs of cards between the remaining fingers. When you are done, she should have four pairs of cards between the fingers of her right hand.

Do the same with her left hand. Put *pairs* of cards between her fingers, but only *one* card between the ring and little finger of her left hand. Say, "Now for the magic. Let me separate the pairs, and put them together again. Watch very carefully." Remove one of the pairs from the right hand. Separate the cards and lay them side by side on the table. Remove another pair, separate it, and lay each card on top of one of the cards on the table. Repeat this with another pair from the right hand. (You are simply making two piles of cards on the table.) Then do the same with the cards from the left hand, until you have only the *one* card remaining.

Point to this single card and tell your helper, "I call this the Acrobat Card because it can do a wonderful trick. The two piles are evenly divided; I will put this single card on one of them. Which pile would you like me to put my Acrobat Card onto?" You drop the card on the pile your helper chooses and continue your patter. "Watch now: the Acrobat Card will jump from this pile to the other one. Alley-oop! Did you see it go?" The helper will say no, of course. You say, "Then I will have to prove to you that it *did* jump.

You pick up the pile that has the odd card. Remove two cards and put them aside, saying, "Here's one of the pairs." Remove two more cards and put them aside, saying, "And here's another pair." Continue until all of the cards have been paired off and discarded. There is no odd card! "It is not in this pile any longer." Turn to the other pile remaining on the table and repeat your previous action of removing cards, two at a time. Amazingly, you end by holding a single card! "Here it is—the Acrobat has arrived!" The single card is tossed onto the table as you leave your audience stunned!

How to Do It

If you practice this trick just as we've described it, you'll soon become good at fooling your audience. Here is some additional advice: Don't show the faces of the cards at any time. People might remember the value of the Acrobat Card and realize it didn't really appear in the other pile.

The Math-a-Magic Secret

Try the trick before you read this explanation. It's amazing. The secret has to do with odds and evens. You have eight spaces between the fingers of both hands. You fill seven of these spaces with pairs of cards. When you make two piles on the table, each pile will have seven cards in it. Seven is an *odd* number, so it doesn't matter which pile you put the one card into because that pile will then have eight cards—an *even* number. You can remove pairs of cards from this pile and none will be left over. The other pile, however, still has only seven cards . . . which makes three pairs plus a single card left over.

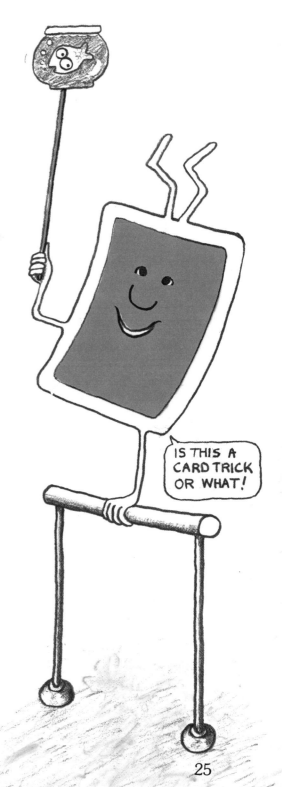

IS THIS A CARD TRICK OR WHAT!

CAN'T YOU COUNT?

The Trick

Can you imagine your best friend not being able to count to ten? Here's how to make it happen. You will need three small objects like coins, pebbles, or pieces of bubble gum. Set them on the table in front of your friend.

"I'm going to teach you to count to ten, using these coins (or whatever objects you have) in a special way. If you pay attention and watch me carefully, you'll learn to do it right away." Pick up the first coin with one hand and say, "one." Pick up the next coin with your *other* hand and say, "two." Pick up the final coin, using the hand you started with, saying, "three." Set the coins back down, alternating hands, as you continue counting, "four, five, six." Now, pick up just *two* coins, one with each hand, counting, "seven, eight." Finally, place the two coins back on the table, one at a time, as you finish counting, "nine, ten!"

Now place the coins in your friend's hands in this way: two coins in one of his hands and one in the other hand. Say, "Here. Were you paying attention? Just count the three coins, one at a time, up to ten. On the count of ten, *all three coins should be down on the table*."

Unless your friend was watching *really* carefully he can try, but he will *never* come out right. He will always reach "eight" holding one coin in his hand and won't be able to finish the count. Of course, there's a trick to it!

How to Do It

If you follow the directions above and practice the counting until you can do it smoothly and quickly, you will fool a lot of people. They won't be able to follow your tricky movements and will think that you have counted the coins in a very simple way. Actually, what

CAN YOU COUNT ON YOUR FRIENDS IF YOUR FRIENDS CAN'T COUNT?

you do is a bit complicated: on your last count, remember, you pick up *two* coins and leave *one* lying on the table. The one on the table is not counted, and you therefore can count the two in your hands to reach ten.

The Math-a-Magic Secret

Some of your friends might be sure they have outfoxed the magician, at last. They will have noticed that you picked up only two coins that last time. But, here is where the math-a-magic secret comes in. It has to do with how the counting *begins*. When *you* do the counting, the three coins start *on the table*. To trick your friend after you show him how to count, you pick up the coins and ask him to hold out his hands. Because you *hand* him the coins, he, like most people, will begin by setting them down on the table. But since he starts wrong, he will always finish wrong! Try it both ways yourself and you'll see—it's mathematically impossible for him to get it right.

Don't be too hard on him for not being able to do the trick. You might suggest, though, that he go back to nursery school, since that's where children learn to count from one to ten! What a nasty thing to say!

THIS IS A REAL NO 'COUNT TRICK!!

SUPER MEMORY

The Trick

Hand a pencil and paper to someone and ask her to write a long number using fifteen digits. Let's pretend she writes: 3 5 6 1 2 9 5 6 3 0 4 1 3 7 3.

Ask her to call the number out slowly, one digit at a time, because you are going to memorize it all! After she's done this, tell her to circle any one digit. Next, ask her to call out all of the other digits, except for the one she circled. But, to confuse you, she can call them out *in any order*, crossing out each one as it is called.

You explain that you will try to remember the original, fifteen-digit number *and* the new, fourteen-digit number. You will then compare the two numbers in your mind and name the digit that she circled. Let's say she calls out: 7 1 3 3 6 2 1 6 3 0 5 5 4 3. When she is done, you think for a moment and say, "You circled the number 9!" And she did!

How to Do It

Perhaps you can do this trick by actually memorizing the numbers and comparing them in your mind. If so, you have an ultra-great memory, far superior to most people's. It is much *easier* to use a trick, but even that will require some "brain work" on your part.

The way you fool your friend is by using *addition*. As she calls out the digits, don't even try to memorize them. Just add them together, one at a time. If you ask her to read the digits slowly, it's not very hard. In our example given above, you would add: $3+5+6+1+2+9+5+6+3+0+4+1+3+7+3$, which equals 58. Remember the total: 58.

When you ask her to call out her smaller, fourteen-digit number, you must again add the digits together. In our example these add up to 49. ($7+1+3+3+6+2+1+6+3+0+5+5+4+3=49$.) Now, you have the totals of the two numbers in your head. The digit that was circled is the remainder left after you subtract the first

MR. SUPER COMPUTER-HEAD KNOWS ALL — SEES ALL — REMEMBERS ALL... THE NUMBER THAT YOU CIRCLED IS...

total from the second total: $58 - 49 = 9$. Now, try it yourself, using a different fifteen-digit number. You are all set to go and wow your friends with your new super memory.

The Math-a-Magic Secret

Most people will hear those long numbers and think of them as just that: long, hard-to-remember numbers. The secret is simply that what your audience *thinks* you are doing (remembering a fifteen-digit number) isn't what you are *actually* doing (adding $7 + 1$, etc.). Don't tell them—let them think you are a genius!

THE POPCORN TRICK

The Trick

Let's say you have a couple of friends over. You're watching television and eating popcorn. You get bored with the program so you suggest doing a trick for them. Here's a great one. Hand your helpers the bowl of popcorn (there must be more than sixty pieces). Turn your back and give them these instructions. (We'll pretend one helper is a boy and one is a girl.)

1 Ask the girl to take any number of pieces of popcorn, between ten and twenty, out of the bowl.

2 Ask the boy to count (silently, so you don't hear) the number the girl took and then to take twice that number of pieces of popcorn out of the bowl for himself.

3 Ask the girl to give the boy four pieces of her popcorn.

4 Finally, ask the boy to count, silently, the number of pieces of popcorn the girl has left and to give her twice that number from his own popcorn. Now you are ready for the trick. Magically, you can tell the boy how many pieces of popcorn he is holding in his hand! In this example, he will have twelve pieces.

The trick looks amazing because you never peek at your helpers. In fact, you can do the entire trick with your eyes closed: they never say anything out loud, you never ask them any questions, and you can do the trick again and again, as long as you keep changing the number in step three!

How to Do It

The secret is the number you ask the girl to give to the boy in step three. Simply multiply this number by *three*; the total is the number of pieces of popcorn the boy is left with at the end! Each time you repeat the trick, simply use a different number at step three. Be sure this number is always under ten (a single-digit number), and that you multiply it by three to get the answer to how many pieces the boy will have. Of course, if your friends keep eating the popcorn, you won't be able to repeat the trick too many times!

STEP ① HERE IS HER HANDFUL.

The Math-a-Magic Secret

At the start of this trick, the girl has a handful of popcorn. But the math-a-magician can think of this handful as *two* groups: There is the popcorn the girl will *keep* and the *four* pieces she will give to the boy.

Let's look at the whole trick this way:

K = the number of pieces the girl gets to keep.

4 = the ones she gives to the boy.

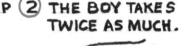

STEP ② THE BOY TAKES TWICE AS MUCH.

STEP ③ GIRL GIVES BOY 4 PIECES, SO NOW SHE HAS

AND HE HAS

STEP ④ BOY GIVES GIRL TWICE THE AMOUNT THAT IS IN HER HAND. SHE HAS K, SO HE GIVES HER K+K.

SHE NOW HAS

AND HE HAS

PRESTO! THE BOY HAS 3 GROUPS OF 4 PIECES. HE HAS 12!

THE MYSTERY OF SIX

The Trick

Give a friend a handful of coins, more than 25 (or any small objects, like buttons or pebbles). Ask her to arrange them in a design that looks like a big number 6. You will have to show her how to do this. When she is finished, it should look like this:

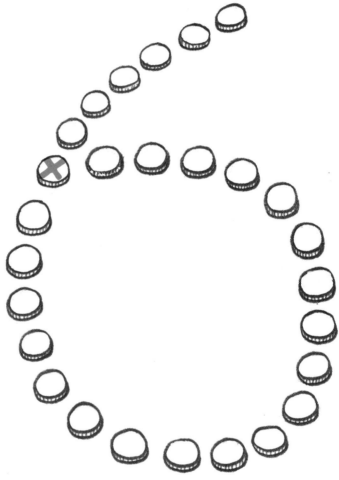

Now, have her think of any number between 10 and 50, but not say it out loud. Explain that when you turn your back, she must count the coins that make up her number, tapping a coin with each count. (Of course, she must count silently!) She is to begin with the coin at the top of the 6 and count downward and around the bottom of the 6, *counterclockwise*. After she reaches the circle part of the 6, she should *only* count the coins in the circle. She will continue to count around and around the circle, until she comes to her secret number. Then she is to *reverse directions* and count to her number one more time, beginning with the *next* coin in the circle. She'll be counting *clockwise* this time. Remind her *not* to count the coins forming the top of the 6, but to stay in the circle at the bottom. Tell her to take her finger off the coin she ends on, and to remember which coin that is. You will now "read her mind" and identify that very coin. And you do!

How to Do It

The best part about this trick is that you don't need to know *anything* about your friend's number. When she forms the 6 (with your help) count how many coins there are in the top part and *add one*. To find the coin she landed on, you are going to count clockwise around the circle that number. But first, take a look at the diagram: the coin that's marked with an X joins the top part of the 6 and the circle. You will start counting *just past* the "joining" coin and count clockwise around the circle. The coin *you* land on will always be the same coin *your friend* landed on!

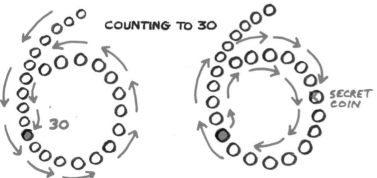

COUNTING TO 30

30

SECRET COIN

WILL SOMEONE GIVE ME A NUMBER?

THANK YOU

I REALLY DON'T NEED THE NUMBER. I JUST WANTED TO BE SURE EVERYONE WAS AWAKE.

33

The Math-a-Magic Secret

If you walk 50 steps in one direction and then turn around and walk 50 steps back, where are you? Right where you started, of course. In the case of The Mystery of Six, counting coins is like taking a walk. When your friend reverses directions in the trick, it's like turning around to walk home. But there's a problem with going home in this trick: You have to stay in the circle instead of walking step-by-step back to where you started.

Look at the example below. Imagine that your "home" has a doorstep and that there are six coins between that doorstep and the circle part of the six.

YOU **WON'T** TAKE THOSE FINAL SEVEN STEPS BACK TO YOUR IMAGINARY DOORSTEP...

BUT YOU **WILL** COUNT OUT SEVEN STEPS **AROUND** THE CIRCLE TO YOUR FRIEND'S SECRET COIN.

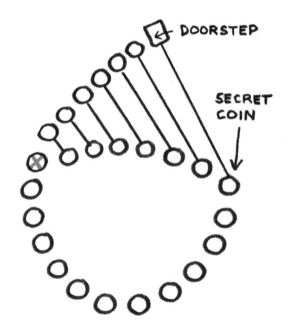

The Trick

Take two pieces of paper, any size, and hand one to a friend. "We will both turn our backs and tear our sheets of paper into smaller pieces," you say. " You can make any number of pieces you wish. In fact, you don't even have to count how many pieces you tear."

You turn your backs to one another and tear up your sheets. "When you are done," you say (with your back still turned) "stack the pieces together and hold them in your hand so I can't see how many there are." You turn and face each other. Now say, "I don't know how many pieces you have in your hand, but I am going to make a prediction. If you count the number of pieces you have, and the total is an *odd* number, I can add my pieces to yours and change the total to an *even* number! But, if your total is an *even* number, then my pieces, added to yours, will make it *odd*!

And it happens! You can do it again and again, and both of you can tear papers into different numbers of pieces each time.

How to Do It

The way to make this math-a-magic trick work is so simple that it's silly, but very few people ever catch on to it. You can tear paper into any number of smaller pieces you wish, but always make it an *odd* number of pieces.

The Math-a-Magic Secret

Think about it a moment. If your friend has an odd number of pieces, your odd number will always make an even total. And, if his or her number is even, your odd number will always make an odd total! Try adding any odd and even numbers together in your head. Now, try adding two odd numbers together. The math-a-magic rule always works!

ODDS AND EVENS

OK, I ADMIT IT! IT'S A TEARABLE TRICK!

35

NIM

WHY DO I ALWAYS WIN? BECAUSE I'M **NIM**-BLE

13, 9 5, 1

The Trick

Nim is a very ancient game that people all over the world play. It is sometimes called "Fifteen" because that is how many objects you need to have. You can use any small objects: rocks, coins, sticks, or pieces of candy, for example. Let's use candy, just to tempt your friend.

Here's how the game is played: Lay the fifteen candies out in a row and explain the rules of Nim to your friend. The two of you will take turns picking up pieces of candy. You each must pick up at least one piece, but you can pick up as many as three on a turn. The object of the game is to leave just one piece of candy for the other person to pick up. Whoever picks up the *last* piece is the loser. And the loser must give the winner all of his candy!

Now, wouldn't it be nice to know that you never have to lose any candy? How is this possible? Because Nim is really a math-a-magic trick. You can always win if you know the secret!

How to Do It

Remember these numbers: 13, 9, 5, 1. These are key numbers that allow you to win. It does not matter who goes first or second, but each time it is *your* turn, you *must* leave one of the key numbers of candies on the table. It's extremely easy to do and, if you follow this rule, you will always win Nim. (Oh, there is one exception. Suppose your opponent read this book too, and he or she knows the winning numbers. Then, the first person who picks up candies will always win because that person can pick up two and leave the losing number of thirteen candies on the table!)

The Math-a-Magic Secret

By making sure that you leave five pieces of candy on your next-to-last turn, you will force your friend to take the last candy. Look at the diagram below to see why. (Remember, the trick is to leave five)

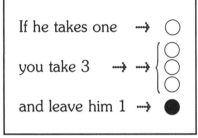

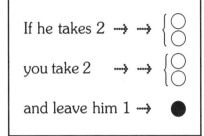

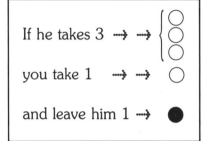

So, if you leave 9, you can have the same control over the game as when you leave 5. With 9 pieces in front of him, your friend would have to take away 4 pieces to get to 5—and that's against the rules. So once again, after he picks 1, 2, or 3, you take just enough to leave 5. Of course, to be absolutely sure of winning, try to be the one who leaves 13 pieces. Why? Well, 13 is 4 pieces more than 9—another 4-piece jump that your friend can't make, just like in the diagram, where the 4-piece jump is from 5 to 1.

So if you leave 13, then you can leave 9.

And if you leave 9, you can leave 5.

And if you leave 5, you can leave 1 and win!

37

A MILLION-DOLLAR BET

GO AHEAD, IT'S EASY!

The Trick

We've got a bet for you. We'll give you a large sheet of newspaper, a double page. Can you fold it in half? It's easy—you can do this without any trouble. Now, fold it in half one more time, in any direction you choose. Again, you can do this easily. But do you think you could fold it in half eight more times? You probably think you could—but watch out! We'll bet you a *million dollars* you can't!

You can make this bet with any person or group. And, believe it or not, they can use any size paper—even a piece that's a mile across! You will never lose your million dollars. In fact, you don't even need a million dollars to offer this bet, because you will always win.

How to Do It

This is a good audience trick because it uses lots of people. All you need is the piece of newspaper and ten prizes. The prizes can be candy or even hundred-dollar bills! Don't worry—you will never lose.

Show your audience the newspaper and explain that you need some help folding it in half. Invite ten people to assist you. Tell the audience that you have chosen ten assistants because that is how many times you want the paper folded in half. Now, ask the assistants to choose the strongest people in the group. Explain that you will have them make the final folds "because those will be the hardest."

Tell the group to stand in a row with the strongest people last. Hand the paper to the first person and ask him to fold it in half. He is then to hand it to the next person to fold in half again. This is to continue, and when the last person folds it in half, you will award all of them their prizes. Imagine how much your audience will enjoy watching "the strongest people" grunt . . . and groan . . . and fail!

The Math-a-Magic Secret

This trick works because of *mathematical progression*, which means a sequence of related numbers. It is easy to understand if you do a little multiplication after each time the paper is folded. Remember, folding something in half is the same as doubling the number of thicknesses, or multiplying by two. Here's how it works:

Fold the paper in half one time (1 thickness $\times 2 = 2$)

Fold it again . . .   ($2 \times 2 = 4$)

A third time . . .   ($4 \times 2 = 8$)

A fourth time . . .   ($8 \times 2 = 16$)

A fifth time . . .   ($16 \times 2 = 32$)

A sixth time . . .   ($32 \times 2 = 64$)

A seventh time . . .   ($64 \times 2 = 128$)

By now, you will find you are having real trouble folding the paper again. It has been getting much smaller and, more importantly, much *thicker* and harder to fold. And, you have only folded it seven times! *If* you can fold it again you'll have 256 thicknesses of paper. You probably will not be able to fold it again, but if you can, you will have 512 thicknesses. *Nobody* can fold it the last time. If you could, the sheet of paper would be *1,024* layers thick!

Try this once and you will understand why you will never lose your million-dollar bet. Now you are ready to trick your friends!

ONLY 4 MORE FOLDS, NO PROBLEM...

NO QUESTIONS ASKED

ADD THESE UP:
1 POUND OF SAWDUST,
1 POUND OF AIR,
1 POUND OF ROCKS,
3 POUNDS OF FAT.
DO YOU HAVE ALL THAT
IN YOUR HEAD?
I THOUGHT SO!

The Trick

This is a really amazing math-a-magic trick. You tell your friend to think of a number. Then you ask her to do a few mathematical things with that number, in her head. You never ask her to say anything out loud. Yet you know what number she is thinking of when the trick is done!

Here's what you do: Tell your friend to think of any *even* number and to remember that number. Now, ask her to double the number she chose. (Of course, she should do this in her head, so that you don't hear.) Now, have her add 12 to the total. Next, ask her to divide this total by 4 and remember the new total. Finally, tell her to take half of the original number and subtract that from the latest total.

You will now "read her mind." Ask her to concentrate on her final number, but pretend to have trouble discovering it. Ask her to close her eyes and think of the number—hard. Have fun! Act as if you are really a mind reader. You're not, but she will always be thinking of 3, and that's the answer you give!

How to Do It

If you do this trick just as it's written, it will always work for you. Of course, you must be sure never to do it for the same person more than once, or they will catch on to the fact that the answer is always 3. The fact that you *never* ask your friend to say anything out loud makes the trick look absolutely impossible. Don't be surprised if she thinks you are a real magician!

The Math-a-Magic Secret

In this problem, you start by asking for an even number. Since later in the trick you ask for the person to subtract half of that number, let's begin by thinking of the number your friend chooses as *two halves* of the whole. For example, start with 18:

(THE EVEN NUMBER)   18

is the same as

$2 \times$ (HALF THE NUMBER)   OR 2×9.

When you double it, you get

$2 \times 2 \times$ (HALF)   OR $2 \times 2 \times 9$

OR $4 \times$ (HALF)   OR 4×9, which is 36.

Now, add 12 to this number.

$4 \times$ (HALF) $+ 12$ OR $36 + 12$.

Now, divide by 4:

$$\frac{4 \times \text{(HALF)}}{4} + \frac{12}{4} \qquad \text{OR } \frac{36}{4} + \frac{12}{4}$$

You get

(HALF) $+ 3$ OR $9 + 3$.

Now, subtract the (HALF) :

(HALF) $+ 3 -$ (HALF)   OR $9 + 3 - 9$.

And there it is:

3   OR 3!

THINK OF A NUMBER.
DOUBLE IT.
ADD 12.
CLOSE YOUR EYES.
DARK, ISN'T IT?

TURN IT AROUND

The Trick

The math-a-magician—that's you—holds up a piece of cardboard, blank side toward the audience. "I'd like to try an experiment with numbers," you say. "I've written four different ones on this piece of cardboard, but I won't show them to you yet. My experiment is to see if you can work together to guess my numbers."

Give a piece of paper and a pencil to someone in the audience. Then explain that he is to write down what you tell him. Ask three other people each to provide a single number. These numbers should be different from each other (and none can be a zero). Ask the person holding the paper to write the numbers down as a single three-digit number. Let's pretend the number is 451.

"I call this my turn-it-around trick," you tell the audience. "so we have to turn the number around. Will you reverse the order of the digits and write the turned-around number underneath, please?"

$$451$$
$$154$$

"Now, subtract the smaller number from the larger number." (In this case, the larger number was the one given by your helpers—but the situation could be reversed.)

$$451$$
$$-\ \underline{154}$$
$$297$$

"Now, take the total, 297, and turn it around again. That makes 792. Add *that* to the total."

$$297$$
$$+\ \underline{792}$$
$$1089$$

"So, using the three selected numbers, we have turned them around twice and have ended with a grand total of 1089. And the amazing part is . . ." you turn your cardboard around . . . "that is the exact same number I wrote before we even started this experiment!"

The audience laughs. The cardboard does *not* show 1089, but instead, 6801. You look at it and appear horrified. Did you make a mistake? You think for a moment while the audience snickers at your error. Then, suddenly, you get an idea. "Oh, I know what went wrong," you explain. "I almost forgot. Remember, I call this my turn-it-around trick?" You smile at the audience as you say, "I just forgot to *turn it around*." You turn the cardboard upside down—and when you do, 6801 becomes 1089!

How to Do It

To prepare the trick, simply write 1089 on a piece of cardboard or paper. The helpers may select any three one-digit numbers at the beginning, but be certain the digits are different from one another and that none of the digits is a zero. The final sum will always be 1089, no matter what the original three numbers are. (Of course, because the answer will always be the same, you can't show the trick to the same audience twice.)

The Math-a-Magic Secret

The secret of this amazing trick is a tough one to follow. But give it a try! Let's say the first number is 467. When we reverse it we get 764. We subtract the smaller from the larger:

$$\begin{array}{r} 764 \\ -\ 467 \end{array}$$

Now, let's look at what will always happen in this situation. (You can make up other examples, which will all work the same way.)

Question: Will we always have to borrow to subtract in the ones column?
Answer: Yes, because the bottom digit is *always* bigger.
Question: Will we always have to borrow to subtract in the tens column?
Answer: Yes, because once we borrow for the ones, the bottom number is *bigger*.
Question: Will the middle numbers always be the same?
Answer: Yes. Now, watch closely:

$$\begin{array}{r} 764 \\ -\ 467 \\ \hline 297 \end{array}$$

What about these ⟶ ↑ ↑
two numbers?
Yes, 9 again: 2 + 7 = 9.

What do you notice about the middle number? It's always 9 (because we borrowed from the tens to do our subtraction in the ones).

The Trick

This is a trick you should show to only one friend at a time. Have *her* do the trick—you will love to watch the expression on her face when it works!

First, lay a piece of black paper on the table. Say, "Will you pretend for a moment that this is 'space?'" Then, on top of the black paper, place several pieces of paper, which you have cut in different shapes. Explain: "This is a magical jig-saw puzzle. Please assemble it so that it makes a rectangle with a hole in the middle." You can help her with this, if she needs it. When it's finished, it will look like the diagram on this page.

"Do you know about black holes in space? They are a great mystery," you say. "Let me show you just how 'puzzling' they can be." You gather up the pieces, turn them over, and wave your hands above them. "All it takes is a few astromagical words: MARS-A-MAGIC... TELESCOPIA... U-F-OZONE... and the trick is done! What? You didn't see the trick? Reassemble the puzzle and you will!" When your friend puts the pieces back together with the *other* side facing up, she will find the diagram on the next page...

THE
BLACK
HOLE

How to Do It

Trace the puzzle shapes from the first illustration onto some colored paper. Do this carefully. Then write the message, "The Black Hole" across the puzzle. Now, paste this onto another piece of paper of a different color (so you can tell the front of the puzzle from the back). Cut the paper along the lines and *throw away the "hole" piece*. Turn the pieces over so the "back side" color shows. Reassemble the pieces the way they are pictured in the second illustration. While holding the pieces together, write the message shown in the second illustration.

You might also want a sheet of black paper to lay the pieces on so the "black hole" shows through. You are now ready to present the trick.

The Math-a-Magic Secret

Actually, the second rectangle, the one without the black hole, is a little bit smaller than the first rectangle. The difference in the two rectangles' sizes is so slight that no one can tell just by looking. But, if you measure the outside edges of both, you can prove it to yourself. When you rearrange the pieces to make the second rectangle, the hole disappears and the rectangle gets smaller. And, if you flip the pieces over and make the hole reappear, the rectangle gets bigger!

WOW! YOU MADE THE BLACK HOLE VANISH!

ABOUT THE AUTHORS

Larry White is the director of the Science Center for the Needham, Massachusetts, schools. Larry's favorite trick is making dollars disappear in an ice cream store. Larry and his wife, Doris, live in Stoughton, Massachusetts.

Ray Broekel lives in Ipswich, Massachusetts with his wife, Peg. He's been writing books and stories since he was in the third grade. His favorite trick is to turn 11 into 2 by cutting the 11 in two with a pair of scissors.

AND ILLUSTRATOR

Meyer Seltzer lives in Chicago with his daughter and their attack cat. He graduated from the School of the Art Institute of Chicago and has illustrated and designed many children's books and textbooks.